Controlled Drugs Register

I0048955

Care Home Name:

Care Home Address:

Date of first entry:

Date of final entry:

Need to keep register for two years after the date of the last entry.

Instructions for the Use of the Controlled Drug Register

All entries must be made in blue or black ink.

Balance checks can be completed in red ink.

If corrections are needed make them as a dated footnote and initial.

The Index

Use the index to record the patient name, medication name and what page it is recorded on in the controlled drugs register.

When a page in the register is complete and more entries are needed use the box to the right to record the next page used.

When a resident is no longer in the home or no longer uses a controlled drug you may put a single line through it on the index page. The item must remain legible.

Pages in the Controlled Drug Register

Each page should be labelled with the resident's name and the name, strength and form of the drug. E.g. Richard Brown MST 10mg Tablets

Guide for Making Entries in the Controlled Drugs Register

Received Items (Ignore administering columns when receiving items)

Amount- The number of dosage units e.g tablets or volume of liquid received

Date- The date received

Signature of the person who received the medication into stock

Running Balance- Add the amount already in stock to the amount that has been received to get the running balance.

Administered Items (Ignore supplied columns when recording administration)

Patient name- record the name of the resident receiving the medication.

Amount given- record dose given i.e. number of units or volume of liquid.

Amount returned- If a medication goes out of date or is no longer needed. Record the amount returned here. Note it is important to comply with the home policy on discarding controlled drugs are they returned to the pharmacy or destroyed in-house?

Given by signature- Signature of the person who gave the medication to the resident

Witnessed signature- signature of the person who witnessed the signature being given.

Running balance- the amount in stock before the administration or discard minus the quantity administered or discarded.

ISBN: 979-8-9930580-0-9

DRUG INDEX

Resident Name:										
Medication Name	PAGE NO									

Resident Name:										
Medication Name	PAGE NO									

Resident Name:										
Medication Name	PAGE NO									

Resident Name:										
Medication Name	PAGE NO									

Resident Name:										
Medication Name	PAGE NO									

Resident Name:										
Medication Name	PAGE NO									

Resident Name:										
Medication Name	PAGE NO									

Resident Name:										
Medication Name	PAGE NO									

Resident Name:										
Medication Name	PAGE NO									

Resident Name:										
Medication Name	PAGE NO									

Resident Name:										
Medication Name	PAGE NO									

Resident Name:										
Medication Name	PAGE NO									

DRUG INDEX

Resident Name:		Resident Name:		Resident Name:	
Medication Name	PAGE NO	Medication Name	PAGE NO	Medication Name	PAGE NO

Resident Name:		Resident Name:		Resident Name:	
Medication Name	PAGE NO	Medication Name	PAGE NO	Medication Name	PAGE NO

Resident Name:		Resident Name:		Resident Name:	
Medication Name	PAGE NO	Medication Name	PAGE NO	Medication Name	PAGE NO

Resident Name:		Resident Name:		Resident Name:	
Medication Name	PAGE NO	Medication Name	PAGE NO	Medication Name	PAGE NO

DRUG INDEX

Resident Name:											
Medication Name	PAGE NO										

Resident Name:											
Medication Name	PAGE NO										

Resident Name:											
Medication Name	PAGE NO										

Resident Name:											
Medication Name	PAGE NO										

Resident Name:											
Medication Name	PAGE NO										

Resident Name:											
Medication Name	PAGE NO										

Resident Name:											
Medication Name	PAGE NO										

Resident Name:											
Medication Name	PAGE NO										

Resident Name:											
Medication Name	PAGE NO										

Resident Name:											
Medication Name	PAGE NO										

Resident Name:											
Medication Name	PAGE NO										

Resident Name:											
Medication Name	PAGE NO										

DRUG INDEX

Resident Name:												
Medication Name	PAGE NO											

Resident Name:												
Medication Name	PAGE NO											

Resident Name:												
Medication Name	PAGE NO											

Resident Name:												
Medication Name	PAGE NO											

Resident Name:												
Medication Name	PAGE NO											

Resident Name:												
Medication Name	PAGE NO											

Resident Name:												
Medication Name	PAGE NO											

Resident Name:												
Medication Name	PAGE NO											

Resident Name:												
Medication Name	PAGE NO											

Name of Service User: Name of Drug:

Amounts Obtained					Amounts Administered or Returned						
Date Received	Amount Received	Name and Address	Received Signature	Date Administered	Time Administered	Amount Given	Amount Returned	Given by signature	Witnessed signature	Balance left in stock

Name of Service User: Name of Drug:

Amounts Obtained				Amounts Administered or Returned						
Date Received	Amount Received	Name and Address	Received Signature	Date Administered	Time Administered	Amount Given	Amount Returned	Given by signature	Witnessed signature	Balance left in stock

Name of Service User: Name of Drug:

Amounts Obtained				Amounts Administered or Returned						
Date Received	Amount Received	Name and Address	Received Signature	Date Administered	Time Administered	Amount Given	Amount Returned	Given by signature	Witnessed signature	Balance left in stock

Name of Service User: Name of Drug:

Amounts Obtained				Amounts Administered or Returned						
Date Received	Amount Received	Name and Address	Received Signature	Date Administered	Time Administered	Amount Given	Amount Returned	Given by signature	Witnessed signature	Balance left in stock

Name of Service User: Name of Drug:

Amounts Obtained				Amounts Administered or Returned						
Date Received	Amount Received	Name and Address	Received Signature	Date Administered	Time Administered	Amount Given	Amount Returned	Given by signature	Witnessed signature	Balance left in stock

Name of Service User: Name of Drug:

Amounts Obtained				Amounts Administered or Returned						
Date Received	Amount Received	Name and Address	Received Signature	Date Administered	Time Administered	Amount Given	Amount Returned	Given by signature	Witnessed signature	Balance left in stock

Name of Service User: Name of Drug:

Amounts Obtained				Amounts Administered or Returned						
Date Received	Amount Received	Name and Address	Received Signature	Date Administered	Time Administered	Amount Given	Amount Returned	Given by signature	Witnessed signature	Balance left in stock

Name of Service User: Name of Drug:

Amounts Obtained				Amounts Administered or Returned						
Date Received	Amount Received	Name and Address	Received Signature	Date Administered	Time Administered	Amount Given	Amount Returned	Given by signature	Witnessed signature	Balance left in stock

Name of Service User: Name of Drug:

Amounts Obtained				Amounts Administered or Returned						
Date Received	Amount Received	Name and Address	Received Signature	Date Administered	Time Administered	Amount Given	Amount Returned	Given by signature	Witnessed signature	Balance left in stock

Name of Service User: Name of Drug:

Amounts Obtained				Amounts Administered or Returned						
Date Received	Amount Received	Name and Address	Received Signature	Date Administered	Time Administered	Amount Given	Amount Returned	Given by signature	Witnessed signature	Balance left in stock

Name of Service User: Name of Drug:

Amounts Obtained					Amounts Administered or Returned						
Date Received	Amount Received	Name and Address	Received Signature		Date Administered	Time Administered	Amount Given	Amount Returned	Given by signature	Witnessed signature	Balance left in stock

Name of Service User: Name of Drug:

Amounts Obtained				Amounts Administered or Returned						
Date Received	Amount Received	Name and Address	Received Signature	Date Administered	Time Administered	Amount Given	Amount Returned	Given by signature	Witnessed signature	Balance left in stock

Name of Service User: Name of Drug:

Amounts Obtained				Amounts Administered or Returned						
Date Received	Amount Received	Name and Address	Received Signature	Date Administered	Time Administered	Amount Given	Amount Returned	Given by signature	Witnessed signature	Balance left in stock

18

Name of Service User: Name of Drug:

Amounts Obtained				Amounts Administered or Returned						
Date Received	Amount Received	Name and Address	Received Signature	Date Administered	Time Administered	Amount Given	Amount Returned	Given by signature	Witnessed signature	Balance left in stock

Name of Service User: Name of Drug:

Amounts Obtained				Amounts Administered or Returned						
Date Received	Amount Received	Name and Address	Received Signature	Date Administered	Time Administered	Amount Given	Amount Returned	Given by signature	Witnessed signature	Balance left in stock

Name of Service User: Name of Drug:

Amounts Obtained				Amounts Administered or Returned						
Date Received	Amount Received	Name and Address	Received Signature	Date Administered	Time Administered	Amount Given	Amount Returned	Given by signature	Witnessed signature	Balance left in stock

Name of Service User: Name of Drug:

Amounts Obtained				Amounts Administered or Returned						
Date Received	Amount Received	Name and Address	Received Signature	Date Administered	Time Administered	Amount Given	Amount Returned	Given by signature	Witnessed signature	Balance left in stock

Name of Service User: Name of Drug:

Amounts Obtained				Amounts Administered or Returned						
Date Received	Amount Received	Name and Address	Received Signature	Date Administered	Time Administered	Amount Given	Amount Returned	Given by signature	Witnessed signature	Balance left in stock

Name of Service User: Name of Drug:

Amounts Obtained				Amounts Administered or Returned						
Date Received	Amount Received	Name and Address	Received Signature	Date Administered	Time Administered	Amount Given	Amount Returned	Given by signature	Witnessed signature	Balance left in stock

Name of Service User: Name of Drug:

Amounts Obtained				Amounts Administered or Returned						
Date Received	Amount Received	Name and Address	Received Signature	Date Administered	Time Administered	Amount Given	Amount Returned	Given by signature	Witnessed signature	Balance left in stock

Name of Service User: Name of Drug:

Amounts Obtained				Amounts Administered or Returned						
Date Received	Amount Received	Name and Address	Received Signature	Date Administered	Time Administered	Amount Given	Amount Returned	Given by signature	Witnessed signature	Balance left in stock

Name of Service User: Name of Drug:

Amounts Obtained				Amounts Administered or Returned						
Date Received	Amount Received	Name and Address	Received Signature	Date Administered	Time Administered	Amount Given	Amount Returned	Given by signature	Witnessed signature	Balance left in stock

Name of Service User: Name of Drug:

Amounts Obtained				Amounts Administered or Returned						
Date Received	Amount Received	Name and Address	Received Signature	Date Administered	Time Administered	Amount Given	Amount Returned	Given by signature	Witnessed signature	Balance left in stock

Name of Service User: Name of Drug:

Amounts Obtained				Amounts Administered or Returned						
Date Received	Amount Received	Name and Address	Received Signature	Date Administered	Time Administered	Amount Given	Amount Returned	Given by signature	Witnessed signature	Balance left in stock

Name of Service User: Name of Drug:

Amounts Obtained					Amounts Administered or Returned						
Date Received	Amount Received	Name and Address	Received Signature		Date Administered	Time Administered	Amount Given	Amount Returned	Given by signature	Witnessed signature	Balance left in stock

Name of Service User: Name of Drug:

Amounts Obtained				Amounts Administered or Returned						
Date Received	Amount Received	Name and Address	Received Signature	Date Administered	Time Administered	Amount Given	Amount Returned	Given by signature	Witnessed signature	Balance left in stock

Name of Service User: Name of Drug:

Amounts Obtained				Amounts Administered or Returned						
Date Received	Amount Received	Name and Address	Received Signature	Date Administered	Time Administered	Amount Given	Amount Returned	Given by signature	Witnessed signature	Balance left in stock

Name of Service User: Name of Drug:

Amounts Obtained				Amounts Administered or Returned						
Date Received	Amount Received	Name and Address	Received Signature	Date Administered	Time Administered	Amount Given	Amount Returned	Given by signature	Witnessed signature	Balance left in stock

Name of Service User: Name of Drug:

Amounts Obtained				Amounts Administered or Returned						
Date Received	Amount Received	Name and Address	Received Signature	Date Administered	Time Administered	Amount Given	Amount Returned	Given by signature	Witnessed signature	Balance left in stock

Name of Service User: Name of Drug:

Amounts Obtained				Amounts Administered or Returned						
Date Received	Amount Received	Name and Address	Received Signature	Date Administered	Time Administered	Amount Given	Amount Returned	Given by signature	Witnessed signature	Balance left in stock

Name of Service User: Name of Drug:

Amounts Obtained				Amounts Administered or Returned						
Date Received	Amount Received	Name and Address	Received Signature	Date Administered	Time Administered	Amount Given	Amount Returned	Given by signature	Witnessed signature	Balance left in stock

Name of Service User: Name of Drug:

Amounts Obtained				Amounts Administered or Returned						
Date Received	Amount Received	Name and Address	Received Signature	Date Administered	Time Administered	Amount Given	Amount Returned	Given by signature	Witnessed signature	Balance left in stock

Name of Service User: Name of Drug:

Amounts Obtained				Amounts Administered or Returned						
Date Received	Amount Received	Name and Address	Received Signature	Date Administered	Time Administered	Amount Given	Amount Returned	Given by signature	Witnessed signature	Balance left in stock

Name of Service User: Name of Drug:

Amounts Obtained				Amounts Administered or Returned						
Date Received	Amount Received	Name and Address	Received Signature	Date Administered	Time Administered	Amount Given	Amount Returned	Given by signature	Witnessed signature	Balance left in stock

Name of Service User: Name of Drug:

Amounts Obtained				Amounts Administered or Returned						
Date Received	Amount Received	Name and Address	Received Signature	Date Administered	Time Administered	Amount Given	Amount Returned	Given by signature	Witnessed signature	Balance left in stock

Name of Service User: Name of Drug:

Amounts Obtained				Amounts Administered or Returned						
Date Received	Amount Received	Name and Address	Received Signature	Date Administered	Time Administered	Amount Given	Amount Returned	Given by signature	Witnessed signature	Balance left in stock

Name of Service User:

Name of Drug:

Amounts Obtained				Amounts Administered or Returned						
Date Received	Amount Received	Name and Address	Received Signature	Date Administered	Time Administered	Amount Given	Amount Returned	Given by signature	Witnessed signature	Balance left in stock

Name of Service User: Name of Drug:

Amounts Obtained				Amounts Administered or Returned						
Date Received	Amount Received	Name and Address	Received Signature	Date Administered	Time Administered	Amount Given	Amount Returned	Given by signature	Witnessed signature	Balance left in stock

Name of Service User: Name of Drug:

Amounts Obtained				Amounts Administered or Returned						
Date Received	Amount Received	Name and Address	Received Signature	Date Administered	Time Administered	Amount Given	Amount Returned	Given by signature	Witnessed signature	Balance left in stock

Name of Service User: Name of Drug:

Amounts Obtained				Amounts Administered or Returned						
Date Received	Amount Received	Name and Address	Received Signature	Date Administered	Time Administered	Amount Given	Amount Returned	Given by signature	Witnessed signature	Balance left in stock

Name of Service User: Name of Drug:

Amounts Obtained				Amounts Administered or Returned						
Date Received	Amount Received	Name and Address	Received Signature	Date Administered	Time Administered	Amount Given	Amount Returned	Given by signature	Witnessed signature	Balance left in stock

Name of Service User: Name of Drug:

Amounts Obtained				Amounts Administered or Returned						
Date Received	Amount Received	Name and Address	Received Signature	Date Administered	Time Administered	Amount Given	Amount Returned	Given by signature	Witnessed signature	Balance left in stock

Name of Service User: Name of Drug:

Amounts Obtained				Amounts Administered or Returned						
Date Received	Amount Received	Name and Address	Received Signature	Date Administered	Time Administered	Amount Given	Amount Returned	Given by signature	Witnessed signature	Balance left in stock

Name of Service User: Name of Drug:

Amounts Obtained				Amounts Administered or Returned						
Date Received	Amount Received	Name and Address	Received Signature	Date Administered	Time Administered	Amount Given	Amount Returned	Given by signature	Witnessed signature	Balance left in stock

Name of Service User: Name of Drug:

Amounts Obtained				Amounts Administered or Returned						
Date Received	Amount Received	Name and Address	Received Signature	Date Administered	Time Administered	Amount Given	Amount Returned	Given by signature	Witnessed signature	Balance left in stock

Name of Service User: Name of Drug:

Amounts Obtained				Amounts Administered or Returned						
Date Received	Amount Received	Name and Address	Received Signature	Date Administered	Time Administered	Amount Given	Amount Returned	Given by signature	Witnessed signature	Balance left in stock

Name of Service User: Name of Drug:

Amounts Obtained				Amounts Administered or Returned						
Date Received	Amount Received	Name and Address	Received Signature	Date Administered	Time Administered	Amount Given	Amount Returned	Given by signature	Witnessed signature	Balance left in stock

Name of Service User: Name of Drug:

Amounts Obtained				Amounts Administered or Returned						
Date Received	Amount Received	Name and Address	Received Signature	Date Administered	Time Administered	Amount Given	Amount Returned	Given by signature	Witnessed signature	Balance left in stock

Name of Service User: Name of Drug:

Amounts Obtained				Amounts Administered or Returned						
Date Received	Amount Received	Name and Address	Received Signature	Date Administered	Time Administered	Amount Given	Amount Returned	Given by signature	Witnessed signature	Balance left in stock

Name of Service User: Name of Drug:

Amounts Obtained				Amounts Administered or Returned						
Date Received	Amount Received	Name and Address	Received Signature	Date Administered	Time Administered	Amount Given	Amount Returned	Given by signature	Witnessed signature	Balance left in stock

Name of Service User: Name of Drug:

Amounts Obtained				Amounts Administered or Returned						
Date Received	Amount Received	Name and Address	Received Signature	Date Administered	Time Administered	Amount Given	Amount Returned	Given by signature	Witnessed signature	Balance left in stock

Name of Service User: Name of Drug:

Amounts Obtained				Amounts Administered or Returned						
Date Received	Amount Received	Name and Address	Received Signature	Date Administered	Time Administered	Amount Given	Amount Returned	Given by signature	Witnessed signature	Balance left in stock

Name of Service User: Name of Drug:

Amounts Obtained				Amounts Administered or Returned						
Date Received	Amount Received	Name and Address	Received Signature	Date Administered	Time Administered	Amount Given	Amount Returned	Given by signature	Witnessed signature	Balance left in stock

58

Name of Service User: Name of Drug:

Amounts Obtained				Amounts Administered or Returned						
Date Received	Amount Received	Name and Address	Received Signature	Date Administered	Time Administered	Amount Given	Amount Returned	Given by signature	Witnessed signature	Balance left in stock

Name of Service User: Name of Drug:

Amounts Obtained				Amounts Administered or Returned						
Date Received	Amount Received	Name and Address	Received Signature	Date Administered	Time Administered	Amount Given	Amount Returned	Given by signature	Witnessed signature	Balance left in stock

Name of Service User: Name of Drug:

Amounts Obtained				Amounts Administered or Returned						
Date Received	Amount Received	Name and Address	Received Signature	Date Administered	Time Administered	Amount Given	Amount Returned	Given by signature	Witnessed signature	Balance left in stock

Name of Service User: Name of Drug:

Amounts Obtained					Amounts Administered or Returned						
Date Received	Amount Received	Name and Address	Received Signature		Date Administered	Time Administered	Amount Given	Amount Returned	Given by signature	Witnessed signature	Balance left in stock

Name of Service User: Name of Drug:

Amounts Obtained				Amounts Administered or Returned						
Date Received	Amount Received	Name and Address	Received Signature	Date Administered	Time Administered	Amount Given	Amount Returned	Given by signature	Witnessed signature	Balance left in stock

Name of Service User: Name of Drug:

Amounts Obtained				Amounts Administered or Returned						
Date Received	Amount Received	Name and Address	Received Signature	Date Administered	Time Administered	Amount Given	Amount Returned	Given by signature	Witnessed signature	Balance left in stock

Name of Service User: Name of Drug:

Amounts Obtained				Amounts Administered or Returned						
Date Received	Amount Received	Name and Address	Received Signature	Date Administered	Time Administered	Amount Given	Amount Returned	Given by signature	Witnessed signature	Balance left in stock

Name of Service User: Name of Drug:

Amounts Obtained				Amounts Administered or Returned						
Date Received	Amount Received	Name and Address	Received Signature	Date Administered	Time Administered	Amount Given	Amount Returned	Given by signature	Witnessed signature	Balance left in stock

Name of Service User: Name of Drug:

Amounts Obtained				Amounts Administered or Returned						
Date Received	Amount Received	Name and Address	Received Signature	Date Administered	Time Administered	Amount Given	Amount Returned	Given by signature	Witnessed signature	Balance left in stock

Name of Service User: Name of Drug:

Amounts Obtained				Amounts Administered or Returned						
Date Received	Amount Received	Name and Address	Received Signature	Date Administered	Time Administered	Amount Given	Amount Returned	Given by signature	Witnessed signature	Balance left in stock

Name of Service User: Name of Drug:

Amounts Obtained				Amounts Administered or Returned						
Date Received	Amount Received	Name and Address	Received Signature	Date Administered	Time Administered	Amount Given	Amount Returned	Given by signature	Witnessed signature	Balance left in stock

Name of Service User: Name of Drug:

Amounts Obtained				Amounts Administered or Returned						
Date Received	Amount Received	Name and Address	Received Signature	Date Administered	Time Administered	Amount Given	Amount Returned	Given by signature	Witnessed signature	Balance left in stock

Name of Service User:　　　　　　　　　　　　　　　　　　　　　　　　Name of Drug:

Amounts Obtained				Amounts Administered or Returned						
Date Received	Amount Received	Name and Address	Received Signature	Date Administered	Time Administered	Amount Given	Amount Returned	Given by signature	Witnessed signature	Balance left in stock

Name of Service User: Name of Drug:

Amounts Obtained					Amounts Administered or Returned						
Date Received	Amount Received	Name and Address	Received Signature		Date Administered	Time Administered	Amount Given	Amount Returned	Given by signature	Witnessed signature	Balance left in stock

Name of Service User: Name of Drug:

Amounts Obtained				Amounts Administered or Returned						
Date Received	Amount Received	Name and Address	Received Signature	Date Administered	Time Administered	Amount Given	Amount Returned	Given by signature	Witnessed signature	Balance left in stock

Name of Service User: Name of Drug:

Amounts Obtained				Amounts Administered or Returned						
Date Received	Amount Received	Name and Address	Received Signature	Date Administered	Time Administered	Amount Given	Amount Returned	Given by signature	Witnessed signature	Balance left in stock

Name of Service User: Name of Drug:

Amounts Obtained				Amounts Administered or Returned						
Date Received	Amount Received	Name and Address	Received Signature	Date Administered	Time Administered	Amount Given	Amount Returned	Given by signature	Witnessed signature	Balance left in stock

Name of Service User: Name of Drug:

Amounts Obtained				Amounts Administered or Returned						
Date Received	Amount Received	Name and Address	Received Signature	Date Administered	Time Administered	Amount Given	Amount Returned	Given by signature	Witnessed signature	Balance left in stock

Name of Service User: Name of Drug:

Amounts Obtained				Amounts Administered or Returned						
Date Received	Amount Received	Name and Address	Received Signature	Date Administered	Time Administered	Amount Given	Amount Returned	Given by signature	Witnessed signature	Balance left in stock

Name of Service User: Name of Drug:

Amounts Obtained				Amounts Administered or Returned						
Date Received	Amount Received	Name and Address	Received Signature	Date Administered	Time Administered	Amount Given	Amount Returned	Given by signature	Witnessed signature	Balance left in stock

Name of Service User: Name of Drug:

Amounts Obtained				Amounts Administered or Returned						
Date Received	Amount Received	Name and Address	Received Signature	Date Administered	Time Administered	Amount Given	Amount Returned	Given by signature	Witnessed signature	Balance left in stock

Name of Service User: Name of Drug:

Amounts Obtained					Amounts Administered or Returned						
Date Received	Amount Received	Name and Address		Received Signature	Date Administered	Time Administered	Amount Given	Amount Returned	Given by signature	Witnessed signature	Balance left in stock

Name of Service User: Name of Drug:

Amounts Obtained				Amounts Administered or Returned						
Date Received	Amount Received	Name and Address	Received Signature	Date Administered	Time Administered	Amount Given	Amount Returned	Given by signature	Witnessed signature	Balance left in stock

Name of Service User: Name of Drug:

Amounts Obtained				Amounts Administered or Returned						
Date Received	Amount Received	Name and Address	Received Signature	Date Administered	Time Administered	Amount Given	Amount Returned	Given by signature	Witnessed signature	Balance left in stock

Name of Service User: Name of Drug:

Amounts Obtained				Amounts Administered or Returned						
Date Received	Amount Received	Name and Address	Received Signature	Date Administered	Time Administered	Amount Given	Amount Returned	Given by signature	Witnessed signature	Balance left in stock

Name of Service User: Name of Drug:

Amounts Obtained				Amounts Administered or Returned						
Date Received	Amount Received	Name and Address	Received Signature	Date Administered	Time Administered	Amount Given	Amount Returned	Given by signature	Witnessed signature	Balance left in stock

Name of Service User: Name of Drug:

Amounts Obtained				Amounts Administered or Returned						
Date Received	Amount Received	Name and Address	Received Signature	Date Administered	Time Administered	Amount Given	Amount Returned	Given by signature	Witnessed signature	Balance left in stock

Name of Service User: Name of Drug:

Amounts Obtained				Amounts Administered or Returned						
Date Received	Amount Received	Name and Address	Received Signature	Date Administered	Time Administered	Amount Given	Amount Returned	Given by signature	Witnessed signature	Balance left in stock

Name of Service User: Name of Drug:

Amounts Obtained				Amounts Administered or Returned						
Date Received	Amount Received	Name and Address	Received Signature	Date Administered	Time Administered	Amount Given	Amount Returned	Given by signature	Witnessed signature	Balance left in stock

Name of Service User: Name of Drug:

Amounts Obtained				Amounts Administered or Returned						
Date Received	Amount Received	Name and Address	Received Signature	Date Administered	Time Administered	Amount Given	Amount Returned	Given by signature	Witnessed signature	Balance left in stock

88

Name of Service User: Name of Drug:

Amounts Obtained				Amounts Administered or Returned						
Date Received	Amount Received	Name and Address	Received Signature	Date Administered	Time Administered	Amount Given	Amount Returned	Given by signature	Witnessed signature	Balance left in stock

Name of Service User: Name of Drug:

Amounts Obtained				Amounts Administered or Returned						
Date Received	Amount Received	Name and Address	Received Signature	Date Administered	Time Administered	Amount Given	Amount Returned	Given by signature	Witnessed signature	Balance left in stock

Name of Service User: Name of Drug:

Amounts Obtained				Amounts Administered or Returned						
Date Received	Amount Received	Name and Address	Received Signature	Date Administered	Time Administered	Amount Given	Amount Returned	Given by signature	Witnessed signature	Balance left in stock

Name of Service User: Name of Drug:

Amounts Obtained				Amounts Administered or Returned						
Date Received	Amount Received	Name and Address	Received Signature	Date Administered	Time Administered	Amount Given	Amount Returned	Given by signature	Witnessed signature	Balance left in stock

Name of Service User: Name of Drug:

Amounts Obtained				Amounts Administered or Returned						
Date Received	Amount Received	Name and Address	Received Signature	Date Administered	Time Administered	Amount Given	Amount Returned	Given by signature	Witnessed signature	Balance left in stock

Name of Service User: Name of Drug:

Amounts Obtained					Amounts Administered or Returned						
Date Received	Amount Received	Name and Address	Received Signature		Date Administered	Time Administered	Amount Given	Amount Returned	Given by signature	Witnessed signature	Balance left in stock

Name of Service User: Name of Drug:

Amounts Obtained				Amounts Administered or Returned						
Date Received	Amount Received	Name and Address	Received Signature	Date Administered	Time Administered	Amount Given	Amount Returned	Given by signature	Witnessed signature	Balance left in stock

Name of Service User: Name of Drug:

Amounts Obtained					Amounts Administered or Returned						
Date Received	Amount Received	Name and Address		Received Signature	Date Administered	Time Administered	Amount Given	Amount Returned	Given by signature	Witnessed signature	Balance left in stock

Name of Service User: Name of Drug:

Amounts Obtained				Amounts Administered or Returned						
Date Received	Amount Received	Name and Address	Received Signature	Date Administered	Time Administered	Amount Given	Amount Returned	Given by signature	Witnessed signature	Balance left in stock

Name of Service User: Name of Drug:

Amounts Obtained				Amounts Administered or Returned						
Date Received	Amount Received	Name and Address	Received Signature	Date Administered	Time Administered	Amount Given	Amount Returned	Given by signature	Witnessed signature	Balance left in stock

Name of Service User: Name of Drug:

Amounts Obtained				Amounts Administered or Returned						
Date Received	Amount Received	Name and Address	Received Signature	Date Administered	Time Administered	Amount Given	Amount Returned	Given by signature	Witnessed signature	Balance left in stock

Name of Service User: Name of Drug:

Amounts Obtained				Amounts Administered or Returned						
Date Received	Amount Received	Name and Address	Received Signature	Date Administered	Time Administered	Amount Given	Amount Returned	Given by signature	Witnessed signature	Balance left in stock

Name of Service User: Name of Drug:

Amounts Obtained				Amounts Administered or Returned						
Date Received	Amount Received	Name and Address	Received Signature	Date Administered	Time Administered	Amount Given	Amount Returned	Given by signature	Witnessed signature	Balance left in stock

Name of Service User: Name of Drug:

Amounts Obtained				Amounts Administered or Returned						
Date Received	Amount Received	Name and Address	Received Signature	Date Administered	Time Administered	Amount Given	Amount Returned	Given by signature	Witnessed signature	Balance left in stock

Name of Service User: Name of Drug:

Amounts Obtained				Amounts Administered or Returned						
Date Received	Amount Received	Name and Address	Received Signature	Date Administered	Time Administered	Amount Given	Amount Returned	Given by signature	Witnessed signature	Balance left in stock

Name of Service User: Name of Drug:

Amounts Obtained				Amounts Administered or Returned						
Date Received	Amount Received	Name and Address	Received Signature	Date Administered	Time Administered	Amount Given	Amount Returned	Given by signature	Witnessed signature	Balance left in stock

Name of Service User: Name of Drug:

Amounts Obtained				Amounts Administered or Returned						
Date Received	Amount Received	Name and Address	Received Signature	Date Administered	Time Administered	Amount Given	Amount Returned	Given by signature	Witnessed signature	Balance left in stock

Name of Service User: Name of Drug:

Amounts Obtained					Amounts Administered or Returned						
Date Received	Amount Received	Name and Address	Received Signature		Date Administered	Time Administered	Amount Given	Amount Returned	Given by signature	Witnessed signature	Balance left in stock

Name of Service User: Name of Drug:

Amounts Obtained				Amounts Administered or Returned						
Date Received	Amount Received	Name and Address	Received Signature	Date Administered	Time Administered	Amount Given	Amount Returned	Given by signature	Witnessed signature	Balance left in stock

Name of Service User: Name of Drug:

Amounts Obtained				Amounts Administered or Returned						
Date Received	Amount Received	Name and Address	Received Signature	Date Administered	Time Administered	Amount Given	Amount Returned	Given by signature	Witnessed signature	Balance left in stock

Name of Service User: Name of Drug:

Amounts Obtained				Amounts Administered or Returned						
Date Received	Amount Received	Name and Address	Received Signature	Date Administered	Time Administered	Amount Given	Amount Returned	Given by signature	Witnessed signature	Balance left in stock

Name of Service User: Name of Drug:

Amounts Obtained					Amounts Administered or Returned						
Date Received	Amount Received	Name and Address	Received Signature		Date Administered	Time Administered	Amount Given	Amount Returned	Given by signature	Witnessed signature	Balance left in stock

Name of Service User: Name of Drug:

Amounts Obtained				Amounts Administered or Returned						
Date Received	Amount Received	Name and Address	Received Signature	Date Administered	Time Administered	Amount Given	Amount Returned	Given by signature	Witnessed signature	Balance left in stock

Name of Service User: Name of Drug:

Amounts Obtained					Amounts Administered or Returned						
Date Received	Amount Received	Name and Address		Received Signature	Date Administered	Time Administered	Amount Given	Amount Returned	Given by signature	Witnessed signature	Balance left in stock

Name of Service User: Name of Drug:

Amounts Obtained				Amounts Administered or Returned						
Date Received	Amount Received	Name and Address	Received Signature	Date Administered	Time Administered	Amount Given	Amount Returned	Given by signature	Witnessed signature	Balance left in stock

Name of Service User: Name of Drug:

Amounts Obtained				Amounts Administered or Returned						
Date Received	Amount Received	Name and Address	Received Signature	Date Administered	Time Administered	Amount Given	Amount Returned	Given by signature	Witnessed signature	Balance left in stock

Name of Service User: Name of Drug:

Amounts Obtained				Amounts Administered or Returned						
Date Received	Amount Received	Name and Address	Received Signature	Date Administered	Time Administered	Amount Given	Amount Returned	Given by signature	Witnessed signature	Balance left in stock

Name of Service User: Name of Drug:

Amounts Obtained				Amounts Administered or Returned						
Date Received	Amount Received	Name and Address	Received Signature	Date Administered	Time Administered	Amount Given	Amount Returned	Given by signature	Witnessed signature	Balance left in stock

Name of Service User: Name of Drug:

Amounts Obtained				Amounts Administered or Returned						
Date Received	Amount Received	Name and Address	Received Signature	Date Administered	Time Administered	Amount Given	Amount Returned	Given by signature	Witnessed signature	Balance left in stock

Name of Service User: Name of Drug:

Amounts Obtained				Amounts Administered or Returned						
Date Received	Amount Received	Name and Address	Received Signature	Date Administered	Time Administered	Amount Given	Amount Returned	Given by signature	Witnessed signature	Balance left in stock

Name of Service User: Name of Drug:

Amounts Obtained				Amounts Administered or Returned						
Date Received	Amount Received	Name and Address	Received Signature	Date Administered	Time Administered	Amount Given	Amount Returned	Given by signature	Witnessed signature	Balance left in stock

Name of Service User: Name of Drug:

Amounts Obtained				Amounts Administered or Returned						
Date Received	Amount Received	Name and Address	Received Signature	Date Administered	Time Administered	Amount Given	Amount Returned	Given by signature	Witnessed signature	Balance left in stock

Name of Service User: Name of Drug:

Amounts Obtained				Amounts Administered or Returned						
Date Received	Amount Received	Name and Address	Received Signature	Date Administered	Time Administered	Amount Given	Amount Returned	Given by signature	Witnessed signature	Balance left in stock

Name of Service User: Name of Drug:

Amounts Obtained				Amounts Administered or Returned						
Date Received	Amount Received	Name and Address	Received Signature	Date Administered	Time Administered	Amount Given	Amount Returned	Given by signature	Witnessed signature	Balance left in stock

Name of Service User: Name of Drug:

Amounts Obtained				Amounts Administered or Returned						
Date Received	Amount Received	Name and Address	Received Signature	Date Administered	Time Administered	Amount Given	Amount Returned	Given by signature	Witnessed signature	Balance left in stock

Name of Service User: Name of Drug:

Amounts Obtained				Amounts Administered or Returned						
Date Received	Amount Received	Name and Address	Received Signature	Date Administered	Time Administered	Amount Given	Amount Returned	Given by signature	Witnessed signature	Balance left in stock

Name of Service User: Name of Drug:

Amounts Obtained				Amounts Administered or Returned						
Date Received	Amount Received	Name and Address	Received Signature	Date Administered	Time Administered	Amount Given	Amount Returned	Given by signature	Witnessed signature	Balance left in stock

Name of Service User: Name of Drug:

Amounts Obtained				Amounts Administered or Returned						
Date Received	Amount Received	Name and Address	Received Signature	Date Administered	Time Administered	Amount Given	Amount Returned	Given by signature	Witnessed signature	Balance left in stock

Name of Service User:

Name of Drug:

Amounts Obtained				Amounts Administered or Returned						
Date Received	Amount Received	Name and Address	Received Signature	Date Administered	Time Administered	Amount Given	Amount Returned	Given by signature	Witnessed signature	Balance left in stock

Name of Service User: Name of Drug:

Amounts Obtained				Amounts Administered or Returned						
Date Received	Amount Received	Name and Address	Received Signature	Date Administered	Time Administered	Amount Given	Amount Returned	Given by signature	Witnessed signature	Balance left in stock

Name of Service User: Name of Drug:

Amounts Obtained				Amounts Administered or Returned						
Date Received	Amount Received	Name and Address	Received Signature	Date Administered	Time Administered	Amount Given	Amount Returned	Given by signature	Witnessed signature	Balance left in stock

Name of Service User: Name of Drug:

Amounts Obtained				Amounts Administered or Returned						
Date Received	Amount Received	Name and Address	Received Signature	Date Administered	Time Administered	Amount Given	Amount Returned	Given by signature	Witnessed signature	Balance left in stock

Name of Service User: Name of Drug:

Amounts Obtained				Amounts Administered or Returned						
Date Received	Amount Received	Name and Address	Received Signature	Date Administered	Time Administered	Amount Given	Amount Returned	Given by signature	Witnessed signature	Balance left in stock

Name of Service User: Name of Drug:

Amounts Obtained				Amounts Administered or Returned						
Date Received	Amount Received	Name and Address	Received Signature	Date Administered	Time Administered	Amount Given	Amount Returned	Given by signature	Witnessed signature	Balance left in stock

Name of Service User: Name of Drug:

Amounts Obtained				Amounts Administered or Returned						
Date Received	Amount Received	Name and Address	Received Signature	Date Administered	Time Administered	Amount Given	Amount Returned	Given by signature	Witnessed signature	Balance left in stock

Name of Service User: Name of Drug:

Amounts Obtained					Amounts Administered or Returned						
Date Received	Amount Received	Name and Address	Received Signature		Date Administered	Time Administered	Amount Given	Amount Returned	Given by signature	Witnessed signature	Balance left in stock

Name of Service User: **Name of Drug:**

Amounts Obtained				Amounts Administered or Returned						
Date Received	Amount Received	Name and Address	Received Signature	Date Administered	Time Administered	Amount Given	Amount Returned	Given by signature	Witnessed signature	Balance left in stock

Name of Service User: Name of Drug:

Amounts Obtained				Amounts Administered or Returned						
Date Received	Amount Received	Name and Address	Received Signature	Date Administered	Time Administered	Amount Given	Amount Returned	Given by signature	Witnessed signature	Balance left in stock

Name of Service User: Name of Drug:

Amounts Obtained				Amounts Administered or Returned						
Date Received	Amount Received	Name and Address	Received Signature	Date Administered	Time Administered	Amount Given	Amount Returned	Given by signature	Witnessed signature	Balance left in stock

Name of Service User: Name of Drug:

Amounts Obtained				Amounts Administered or Returned						
Date Received	Amount Received	Name and Address	Received Signature	Date Administered	Time Administered	Amount Given	Amount Returned	Given by signature	Witnessed signature	Balance left in stock

Name of Service User: Name of Drug:

Amounts Obtained				Amounts Administered or Returned						
Date Received	Amount Received	Name and Address	Received Signature	Date Administered	Time Administered	Amount Given	Amount Returned	Given by signature	Witnessed signature	Balance left in stock

Name of Service User: Name of Drug:

Amounts Obtained				Amounts Administered or Returned						
Date Received	Amount Received	Name and Address	Received Signature	Date Administered	Time Administered	Amount Given	Amount Returned	Given by signature	Witnessed signature	Balance left in stock

Name of Service User: Name of Drug:

Amounts Obtained				Amounts Administered or Returned						
Date Received	Amount Received	Name and Address	Received Signature	Date Administered	Time Administered	Amount Given	Amount Returned	Given by signature	Witnessed signature	Balance left in stock

Name of Service User: Name of Drug:

Amounts Obtained					Amounts Administered or Returned						
Date Received	Amount Received	Name and Address	Received Signature		Date Administered	Time Administered	Amount Given	Amount Returned	Given by signature	Witnessed signature	Balance left in stock

Name of Service User: Name of Drug:

Amounts Obtained				Amounts Administered or Returned						
Date Received	Amount Received	Name and Address	Received Signature	Date Administered	Time Administered	Amount Given	Amount Returned	Given by signature	Witnessed signature	Balance left in stock

Name of Service User: Name of Drug:

Amounts Obtained				Amounts Administered or Returned						
Date Received	Amount Received	Name and Address	Received Signature	Date Administered	Time Administered	Amount Given	Amount Returned	Given by signature	Witnessed signature	Balance left in stock

Name of Service User: Name of Drug:

Amounts Obtained				Amounts Administered or Returned						
Date Received	Amount Received	Name and Address	Received Signature	Date Administered	Time Administered	Amount Given	Amount Returned	Given by signature	Witnessed signature	Balance left in stock

Name of Service User: Name of Drug:

Amounts Obtained					Amounts Administered or Returned						
Date Received	Amount Received	Name and Address	Received Signature	Date Administered	Time Administered	Amount Given	Amount Returned	Given by signature	Witnessed signature	Balance left in stock

Name of Service User: Name of Drug:

Amounts Obtained				Amounts Administered or Returned						
Date Received	Amount Received	Name and Address	Received Signature	Date Administered	Time Administered	Amount Given	Amount Returned	Given by signature	Witnessed signature	Balance left in stock

Name of Service User:

Name of Drug:

Amounts Obtained				Amounts Administered or Returned						
Date Received	Amount Received	Name and Address	Received Signature	Date Administered	Time Administered	Amount Given	Amount Returned	Given by signature	Witnessed signature	Balance left in stock

Name of Service User: Name of Drug:

Amounts Obtained				Amounts Administered or Returned						
Date Received	Amount Received	Name and Address	Received Signature	Date Administered	Time Administered	Amount Given	Amount Returned	Given by signature	Witnessed signature	Balance left in stock

Name of Service User: Name of Drug:

Amounts Obtained					Amounts Administered or Returned						
Date Received	Amount Received	Name and Address		Received Signature	Date Administered	Time Administered	Amount Given	Amount Returned	Given by signature	Witnessed signature	Balance left in stock

www.ingramcontent.com/pod-product-compliance
Lightning Source LLC
Chambersburg PA
CBHW041059210326

41597CB00004B/138